Sexual Harassment in Education

John F. Lewis, Susan C. Hastings,
Anne C. Morgan

NATIONAL ORGANIZATION ON LEGAL PROBLEMS OF EDUCATION

Copyright © 1992
Squire, Sanders & Dempsey
ISBN 1-56534-057-4

Published by

NATIONAL ORGANIZATION ON LEGAL PROBLEMS OF EDUCATION
3601 S.W. 29th Street, Suite 223
Topeka, Kansas 66614
(913) 273-3550 • Fax (913) 273-2001

About the Authors

John F. Lewis is the Managing Partner of the Cleveland office of Squire, Sanders & Dempsey. He has specialized in education law for the past twenty-five years and is Past President of the National Organization on Legal Problems in Education (NOLPE). In addition to co-authoring Baldwin's Ohio School Law (1976-1991), he co-authored Ohio Collective Bargaining Law (1983). He has contributed articles to numerous legal periodicals and has lectured nationally on various education law topics. He currently serves as a Trustee of Case Western Reserve University. A graduate of Eastbourne College, Sussex, England, and Amherst College from which he received his B.A. degree in 1955, Mr. Lewis holds a Juris Doctor from the University of Michigan awarded in 1958.

Susan C. Hastings is an Associate in the Cleveland office of Squire, Sanders & Dempsey specializing in public and private sector labor and employment law. She has represented boards of education in all facets of labor and employment matters, including teaching and nonteaching contract negotiations, arbitrations, termination proceedings, administrative hearings, court appeals of administrative orders, civil actions arising in federal and state courts, and special education matters. She also has advised private and public sector employers with regard to legal issues and obligations relating to civil rights and discrimination arising under Title VII, the Americans with Disabilities Act, Section 504 of the Vocational Rehabilitation Act, Title IX, and the Ohio Fair Employment Practice Act, including sex discrimination and sexual harassment. She joined the firm in 1985 upon graduation from the University of Iowa Law School from which she earned her Juris Doctor. Ms. Hastings' undergraduate degree, also awarded by the University of Iowa, was received in 1980.

Anne C. Morgan is an Associate in the Cleveland office of Squire, Sanders & Dempsey specializing in education, discrimination and labor law. She joined the firm in 1990 upon graduation from Case Western University School of Law from which she earned her Juris Doctor. Ms. Morgan's undergraduate degree awarded by the University of Michigan was received in 1986.

TABLE OF CONTENTS

I. Introduction

"Sexual harassment" are the buzzwords of the 90's. The words moved to center stage with the Supreme Court confirmation hearings of Justice Clarence Thomas and the allegations by Anita Hill that she had been sexually harassed. The hearings underscored the complexity of this emotionally charged issue. As in most workplaces, sexual harassment has been an issue of significant magnitude in educational institutions as well. It has left the education community asking, "What is sexual harassment?" "What remedies exist for it?" "How can an educational institution prevent harassment and avoid liability?" "What obligations does an institution have to an accused harasser and to the victim?" "Does the analysis differ with the identity of the victim and the identity of the alleged harasser, e.g., student, faculty member, custodian?"

This monograph answers the foregoing questions and focuses on the legal issues surrounding sexual harassment as they confront educational institutions on a daily, often imperceptible, basis. It also provides practical guidance for institutions in developing and implementing policies and procedures for addressing sexual harassment.

II. Myths About Sexual Harassment

Myth 1: If our institution had a sexual harassment problem, we would have heard about it.

Fact: Research indicates that victims of sexual harassment do not freely report sexual harassment nor are they encouraged to do so. A policy and procedure for dealing with such complaints can open the lines of communication encouraging victims to report harassment without fear of repercussions.

Myth 2: Institutions can be liable only for sexual harassment of staff by administrators and/or students by employees.

Answer: Sexual harassment can occur between co-workers, an employee and a student, and between students. Individual board members and employees may be personally liable for sexual harassment as well as the institution.

Myth 3: An administrator hears a rumor from a reliable source that Teacher X propositioned a student. Since the administrator never saw the teacher do it and no one formally reported such behavior, the best thing to do is ignore the situation and it will go away.

Answer: While institutions must protect the privacy and other rights of an alleged harasser, some response is necessary even if an incident has not been formally reported. Institutions who are aware or should be aware that a problem exists, but fail investigate or stop the harassment, may be held liable.

Myth 4: Boys will be boys. Institutions need only concern themselves with blatant forms of sexual harassment and may turn the other cheek with respect to peer harassment between students.

Answer: Educational institutions can no longer ignore even the most innocuous behavior of its students which may be construed as sexual harassment including, for example, jokes about girls or women, bra snapping, bathroom wall graffiti and name-calling. Institutions and educators must take an active role to prevent and halt such behavior, or face a real threat of liability.

III. FEDERAL LAWS GOVERNING SEXUAL HARASSMENT IN EDUCATIONAL INSTITUTIONS

Sexual harassment involving public educational institutions and educators is governed by the laws affecting all public, federally funded, entities such as Title VII of the Civil Rights Act and 42 U.S.C. section 1983. Additionally, sexual harassment of employees and students in federally funded programs is regulated by Title IX of the Education Amendments of 1974. These federal laws have been interpreted to allow the full range of remedies against educators and institutions, including compensatory and punitive damages. (See Appendix A).

IV. RELATED STATE LEGISLATION

Most states have civil rights statutes which govern discrimination, including sexual harassment, in both public and private sector employment. Indeed, some states have adopted statutes specifically governing sexual harassment in employment.[1]

Several states have gone one step further by creating statutes which govern sexual harassment in education. In Minnesota, for example, sexual harassment is specifically prohibited in senior high and post-secondary schools.[2] Similarly, California, Illinois and Wisconsin prohibit sexual harassment in education and/or higher education.[3] Likewise, on April 15, 1992, the Iowa state legislature passed a bill which prohibits sexual harassment of state employees and persons attending state educational institutions.[4] The Connecticut state legislature followed suit on May 27, 1992 by approving several bills relating to sexual harassment on campus and in higher education, empowering a commission to require employers to take proactive steps with regard to sexual harassment in the workplace.[5]

---

1. Examples of state statutory measures taken with regard to sexual harassment in employment include ALASKA STAT. § 23.10.440 (1992) (requires employers to post information regarding sexual harassment); CONN. GEN. STAT. § 46a-60 (1990) (defines "sexual harassment" as a discriminatory employment practice; ILL. REV. STAT. ch. 68, ¶¶ 2-101, 2-102 (1992) (defining sexual harassment as a civil rights violation in employment); ME. REV. STAT. § 807 (1991) (requires posting regarding sexual harassment in the workplace as well as education and training for workers regarding sexual harassment); MICH. COMP. LAWS § 37.2103 (1991) (sexual harassment is discrimination); MINN. STAT. § 363.01, *et seq.* (1992) (sexual harassment as a civil rights violation); N. D. CENT. CODE § 14-02.4-02 (1991) (definition of "discriminatory practice" includes sexual harassment); WIS. STAT. §§ 111.32, 111.36 (1989-1990) (defining and prohibiting sexual harassment in employment).

2. MINN. STAT. §§ 127.46 and 135A.15 (1991).

3. CAL. EDUC. CODE §§ 212, 212.5 and 230 (1992) (defining and prohibiting sexual harassment in education); ILL. REV. STAT. ch. 68, ¶ 1-102 (1992) (declaring policy of the state to be, in part, the prevention of "sexual harassment in employment and...in higher education"); ILL. REV. STAT. ch. 68, ¶¶ 5A-101, 5A-102 (1992) (defining sexual harassment as a civil rights violation in higher education); ILL. REV. STAT. ch. 144, ¶ 189-21 (1992) (creating reporting and other requirements regarding sexual harassment for institutions of higher education); WIS. STAT. §§ 36.11 and 38.12 (1989-1990) (creating affirmative duties on the part of the board of regents and district school boards including reporting and education regarding sexual harassment).

4. *See* Senate File 316.

5. *See* Conn. Substitute House Bill Nos. 5601 and 5827, Public Act Nos. 92-83 and 92-85 creating, replacing and amending CONN. GEN. STAT. §§ 10a-55a, *et seq.* and 46a-54, *et seq.*

V. SEXUAL HARASSMENT OF EMPLOYEES IN EDUCATION

A. Sexual Harassment Is Discrimination Under Title VII

Sexual harassment is a recognized form of discrimination prohibited by Title VII of the Civil Rights Act of 1964, as amended, 42 U.S.C. section 2000e, *et seq.*, which provides in part:

> It shall be an unlawful employment practice for an employer—
>
> (1) to fail or refuse to hire or to discharge any individual, or otherwise to discriminate against any individual with respect to his compensation, terms, conditions, or privileges of employment, because of such individual's race, color, religion, sex or national origin; or
>
> (2) to limit, segregate or classify his employees or applicants for employment in any way which would deprive or tend to deprive any individual of employment opportunities or otherwise adversely affect his status as an employee, because of such individual's race, color, religion, sex, or national origin.[6]

Any questions that may have existed as to whether sexual harassment was a form of discrimination were dispelled over a decade ago, when the the Equal Employment Opportunity Commission (EEOC) issued guidelines defining sexual harassment as a prohibited form of sex discrimination under Title VII. This view was subsequently endorsed by the Supreme Court.[7] It was not until recently, however, that the finer issues relating to sexual harassment came to the fore. Educators have largely ignored the law of sexual harassment which has been evolving for the past twelve years. They must now deal with it.

B. What Is Sexual Harassment for Purposes of Title VII?

Defining "sexual harassment" is easier than identifying it in the real world. Each situation depends on the facts of the particular case.

---

6. 42 U.S.C. § 2000e-2.
7. Meritor Sav. Bank v. Vinson, 477 U.S. 57 (1986).

In its simplest sense, sexual harassment occurs when an employee is harassed because of his or her sex, male or female.[8] Conduct can constitute sexual harassment even though it is not overtly sexual such as fondling or touching. For example, verbal abuse, pornography or perpetuation of sex-based stereotypes also may be considered sexual harassment.

Moreover, men can be sexually harassed by women based upon the same rationale.[9] For example, where a male employee is heckled by his female boss because she resents working with a man, her conduct is sex-based harassment in violation of Title VII.[10] Likewise, harassment of a male employee by another male may be sexual harassment if it is based on sex.[11]

The EEOC regulations identify three categories of conduct which are deemed to be prohibited sexual harassment under federal law:

> Unwelcome sexual advances, requests for sexual favors, and other verbal and physical conduct of a sexual nature constitute sexual harassment when:
>
> (1) submission to such conduct is made either explicitly or implicitly a term or condition of an individual's employment;

---

8. Hicks v. Gates Rubber Co., 833 F.2d 1406 (10th Cir. 1987); McKinney v. Dole, 765 F.2d 1129 (D.C. Cir. 1985).

9. *See, e.g.*, Nelson v. Reisher, 878 F.2d 1430 (4th Cir. 1989).

10. The same principles apply to harassment based on other protected characteristics, such as race, religion, or national origin. *See, e.g.*, Erebia v. Chrysler Plastic Prods. Corp., 772 F.2d 1250 (6th Cir. 1985), *cert. denied*, 475 U.S. 1015 (1986) (racial hostile work environment claim); Torres v. County of Oakland, 758 F.2d 147, 152 (6th Cir. 1985) (national origin hostile environment claim); Cariddi v. Kansas City Chiefs Football Club, 568 F.2d 87 (8th Cir. 1977); Firefighters Inst. for Racial Equality v. St. Louis, 549 F.2d 506 (8th Cir.), *cert. denied sub nom.*, Banta v. United States, 434 U.S. 819 (1977), Compston v. Borden, Inc., 424 F. Supp. 157 (S.D. Ohio 1976).

11. *See* Morgan v. Massachusetts Gen. Hosp., 901 F.2d 186 (1st Cir. 1990) (male employee complained another male, purportedly homosexual, looked at his "privates" in the restroom, "hung around him a lot," stood behind the employee as he was mopping, causing him to bump into the co-worker, and asked the employee to dance with him at a Christmas party — the court rejected his claims because the conduct complained of was neither sufficiently severe nor adequately pervasive to amount to the type of conduct deemed to be actionable under Title VII). *Cf.* Dillon v. Frank, Postmaster Gen., 58 Empl. Prac. Dec. (CCH) ¶ 41,332 (6th Cir. January 15, 1992) (male post office employee failed to state a claim under Title VII for hostile working environment sexual harassment "based on sex" where he alleged severe harassment and sexual epithets by other male employees directed at his perceived sexual orientation (homosexual) instead of directed at his sex, male).

> (2) submission to or rejection of such conduct by an individual is used as the basis for employment decisions affecting such individual, or
>
> (3) such conduct has the purpose or effect of unreasonably interfering with an individual's work performance or creating an intimidating, hostile, or offensive working environment.[12]

Sexual harassment, thus, is separated into two types of harassment: *quid pro quo* and environmental. The former occurs when submission to or rejection of sexual conduct by an individual is used as the basis for employment decisions affecting that individual. The latter includes unwelcome sexual conduct that unreasonably interferes with an individual's job performance or creates an intimidating, hostile or offensive working environment. (See Appendix B). While *quid pro quo* and environmental harassment are theoretically distinct claims, the line between them is not always clear. For example, a supervisor who makes sexual advances toward a subordinate employee (environmental) may communicate an implicit threat to adversely affect the individual's job status if he/she does not comply (*quid pro quo*).

1. *Quid Pro Quo* Harassment

Quid pro quo harassment is easily recognizable and does not rest on the subtleties and nuances of the hostile environment harassment. The elements of a *quid pro quo* cause of action are:

(1) The employee is a member of a protected class;

(2) The employee was subjected to unwelcomed sexual harassment in the form of sexual advances or requests for sexual favors;

(3) The harassment complained of was based on sex;

(4) The employee's submission to the unwelcomed advances was an express or implied condition for receiving job benefits or the employee's refusal to submit resulted in a tangible job detriment; and

(5) The existence of *respondeat superior* liability.[13]

---

12. 29 C.F.R. § 1604.11(a)(1)-(3).

13. *See, e.g.*, Chamberlin v. 101 Realty, Inc., 915 F.2d 777 (1st Cir. 1990); Highlander v. K.F.C. Nat'l Management Co., 805 F.2d 644, 648 (6th Cir. 1986).

Quid pro quo harassment arises in the education setting where, for example, a male with influence over tenure or other employment decisions approaches a nontenured female professor or teacher for a sexual relationship in exchange for tenure or coupled with the threat of retaliation.[14] A single incident of "*quid pro quo*" is enough to establish a violation. Moreover, an employee can prove such harassment despite the fact that the adverse employment action did not take place until several months after the harassment. For example, passage of a two and one-half month interval between a supervisor's sexual advances and a female employee's discharge may not preclude a finding that the discharge was a consequence of spurned sexual advances and, thus, actionable sexual harassment.[15]

Educators and institutions may successfully rebut a *prima facie* case of *quid pro quo* sexual harassment with evidence that its action taken with respect to an employee was not based on sex. For example, an institution may establish that an employee's rejection of her supervisor's advances does not affect a tangible or economic aspect of her employment. In one case, an employer rebutted an employee's allegations with evidence that her supervisor never mentioned sex in connection with a potential promotion and, further, another employee who succumbed to sexual advances of the supervisor received a promotion based upon merit.[16] An institution may also defend itself by showing the employee's job duties or other conditions of employment did not change after she spurned the alleged advances of her supervisor.[17]

2. Hostile Environment Harassment

Institutions may be liable for sexual harassment which creates an intimidating, abusive or hostile environment regardless of any economic impact on the employee.[18] Environmental harassment must be "sufficiently severe or pervasive to alter the conditions of [the vic-

---

14. *See, e.g.*, University of Pa. v. EEOC, 493 U.S. 182, 185 (1990) (nontenured professor said department chairman sexually harassed her and after she insisted their relationship remain professional only, he submitted a negative letter to the committee responsible for tenure decisions); King v. Board of Regents, 898 F.2d 533 (7th Cir.), *reh'g en banc denied*, 1990 U.S. App. LEXIS 7081 (7th Cir. 1990) (discrimination against nontenured professor).

15. Chamberlin v. 101 Realty, Inc., 915 F.2d 777 (1st Cir. 1990).

16. Spencer v. General Elec. Co., 894 F.2d 651 (4th Cir. 1990).

17. *See, e.g.*, Dockter v. Rudolf Wolff Futures, Inc., 913 F.2d 456 (7th Cir. 1990).

18. Meritor Sav. Bank v. Vinson, 477 U.S. 57 (1986).

tim's] employment and create an abusive working environment" and need not cause "economic" or "tangible" injury.[19]

The elements of hostile environment harassment in many jurisdictions are as follows:

(1) the employee is a member of a protected class;

(2) the employee was subjected to unwelcomed sexual harassment in the form of sexual advances, requests for sexual favors, or other verbal or physical conduct of a sexual nature;

(3) the harassment complained of was based on sex;

(4) the charged sexual harassment had the effect of unreasonably interfering with the employee's work performance and creating an intimidating, hostile, or offensive working environment that affected seriously the psychological well-being of the employee; and

(5) there is *respondeat superior* liability on the employer's part.[20]

Hostile environment cases are not subject to easy rules but, rather, they are fact intensive. A slight variance in fact pattern may sway a particular case one way or the other. For example, in a recent case an elementary school teacher failed to state a *prima facie* case of environmental harassment where she alleged the school's principal "asked her out for a drink", requested her to perform secretarial tasks, and attacked her during a discussion in his office by striking her face and throwing her against a wall. The court found she had alleged a hostile workplace, but failed to allege a pervasively hostile workplace based upon sex.[21]

On the other hand, evidence of a hostile work environment is shown where a male transportation supervisor frequently uses vulgar language, tells sexual jokes around the bus garage, regularly pats or attempts to pat his female employees on the buttocks and, on more than one occasion, touches their breasts.[22] Similarly, where a medical student was subjected to ongoing and pervasive harassment, includ-

---

19. *Id.* at 67.

20. Rabidue v. Osceola Refining Co., 805 F.2d 611, 619-20 (6th Cir. 1986). *Accord* Brooms v. Regal Tube Co., 881 F.2d 412 (7th Cir. 1989); Scandinavian Health Spa, Inc. v. Ohio Civil Rights Comm'n, No. 56593, 1990 Ohio App. LEXIS 757 (Cuyahoga Cty. App. 1990). *But see* Ellison v. Brady, 924 F.2d 872 (9th Cir. 1991).

21. Cobbins v. School Bd. of the City of Lynchburg, Virginia, United States Court of Appeals for the Fourth Circuit, Case No. 90-1754 (January 14, 1991).

22. *See* Comeau v. Board of Educ. of the Ballston Spa Cent. Sch. Dist., 160 A.D.2d 1150, 554 N.Y.S.2d 359 (N.Y. App. Div. April 19, 1990).

ing demeaning sexual comments (e.g., menstruating women are "in heat" and not competent to perform surgery), trivial assignments, and offers of "protection" against harassment in exchange for sex, she was subjected to actionable sexual harassment.[23]

a. *Unwelcomeness*

A portion of the inquiry in hostile environment cases is whether the alleged sexual advances were "unwelcome". Educators should note that a victim's participation in such actions generally will not refute "unwelcomeness"; for example, sexual advances upon an employee by her supervisor are not welcome by virtue of her agreement to submit to sex after he threatens to have her fired.[24] Moreover, harassment may be unwelcome even though a female employee occasionally responds in kind to a barrage of sexual remarks and gestures.[25] In fact, evidence that an employee never verbally rejected her supervisor's demands, but otherwise resisted his advances, will suffice to establish "unwelcomeness".[26] Finally, the victim's sexually provocative speech or dress may be relevant to the inquiry regarding "unwelcomeness", however, courts will consider such evidence only after strongly considering the potential of unfair prejudice to the victim.[27]

b. *Severe or Pervasive*

Hostile environment harassment must be "sufficiently severe or pervasive" to alter the conditions of the victim's employment and create an abusive working environment. While this determination can be made only from the facts on a case-by-case basis, the victim is almost always required to show more than a single incident or comment. For example, where an employee is subjected to only two comments in almost three years, the harassment is not sufficiently severe or pervasive to create a discriminatorily hostile environment.[28] In fact, the incidence of harassment may be required to occur with some frequency before it is actionable. An employee, however, need not subject herself to an extended period of demeaning and degrading provocation

---

23. Lipsett v. University of P. R., 864 F.2d 881 (1st Cir. 1988).
24. Meritor Sav. Bank v. Vinson, 477 U.S. 57, 68. *See, e.g.*, Westmoreland Coal Co. v. West Virginia Human Rights Comm'n, 382 S.E.2d 561 (W. Va. 1989).
25. *See, e.g.*, Wyerick v. Bayou Steel Corp., 887 F.2d 1271 (5th Cir. 1989).
26. *See, e.g.*, Chamberlain v. 101 Realty, 915 F.2d 777 (1st Cir. 1990).
27. Meritor Sav. Bank v. Vinson, 477 U.S. 57 (1986).
28. Keziah v. W.M. Brown & Son, Inc., 888 F.2d 322 (4th Cir. 1989).

before being entitled to seek relief under Title VII. Where an employee experiences "two kisses, three arm strokes," several degrading epithets, and other objectionable conduct over a two-week period, she has been sexually harassed.[29]

The EEOC has taken the position that "sexual flirtation or innuendo, even vulgar language that is trivial or merely annoying" will not normally establish a hostile working environment in violation of the law.[30] However, when conduct reaches the point that the employee is continually subjected to demeaning and offensive language by her supervisor before her colleagues, it necessarily alters the conditions of her employment because it makes her feel unwanted or uncomfortable, and in extreme cases can severely affect the employee's emotional and psychological ability.[31]

Disparaging remarks regarding an employee's pregnancy can constitute sexual harassment. During the course of one employee's pregnancy, her supervisors called her a "dog" and a "whore", and told her "that's what you get for sleeping without your underwear."[32] One of the same supervisors offered another employee money and an apartment if she would "give him [her] body."[33] He also made offensive references to her body, male genitalia, and oral sex.[34] These actions were severe and pervasive enough to constitute hostile environment harassment.

In another case where a supervisor made numerous explicit racial and sexual remarks to a woman, showed her pornographic photographs depicting an interracial act of sodomy and a racial act of bestiality, told her that the photograph showed the "talent" of a black woman, and stated she was hired for the purpose indicated in the photograph, such conduct was also severe and pervasive enough to be considered hostile environment sexual harassment.[35]

c. Reasonableness

The standard for determining whether conduct is sufficiently severe or pervasive to constitute sexual harassment is, in many juris-

---

29. Carrero v. New York City Hous. Auth., 890 F.2d 569 (2d Cir. 1989).

30. *EEOC Policy Guidance to Field Office Personnel*, March 19, 1990, 13 L.R.R.M. 397 (April 2, 1990) [hereinafter "EEOC Guidelines"].

31. Volk v. Coler, 638 F. Supp. 1555, 1558 (C.D. Ill. 1986), *aff'd in part*, 845 F.2d 1422 (7th Cir. 1988).

32. EEOC v. Hacienda Hotel, 881 F.2d 1504 (9th Cir. 1989).

33. *Id.*

34. *Id.* at 1507-08.

35. Brooms v. Regal Tube Co., 881 F.2d 412, 420 (7th Cir. 1989).

dictions, an objective one based on reasonableness. The objective test asks the question of whether a reasonable employee under the victim's circumstances would consider this to be a hostile working environment in violation of Title VII.[36]

Other jurisdictions have adopted a combination of objective and subjective inquiries to determine whether questionable conduct rises to the level of sexual harassment. The dual inquiry incorporates a consideration of the reasonable person or employee, and the particular victim under the circumstances:

> [A] district court must employ a dual standard when evaluating a Title VII sexual harassment claim, considering the likely effect of a defendant's conduct upon a reasonable person's ability to perform his or her work and upon his or her well-being, as well as the actual effect upon the particular plaintiff bringing the claim. Only if the court concludes that the conduct would adversely affect the work performance and the well-being of both a reasonable person and the particular plaintiff bringing the action may it find that the defendant has violated the plaintiff's Title VII rights.[37]

In addition, if the employee voluntarily resigns in the face of unexecuted threats, the harassment is sufficiently pervasive and severe if a reasonable person would have felt compelled to quit under the circumstances.[38]

The newest addition to the reasonableness standard arises in the Eighth Circuit where an Iowa district court has refused to find the alleged victim was subjected to hostile environment harassment, despite its finding that a reasonable person would have considered the particular harassing acts to be "sufficiently severe and pervasive to alter the conditions of that person's employment and create an abusive working environment."[39] The alleged victim's employer talked to her repeatedly about sex, showed her pictures from Penthouse magazine, tried to get her to go out with him, invited her to his apartment

---

36. *See, e.g.,* Ellison v. Brady, 924 F.2d 872 (9th Cir. 1991) (applying a "reasonable woman" standard for determining whether conduct meets the hostile environment criteria); *accord* Andrews v. City of Philadelphia, 895 F.2d 1469 (3d Cir. 1991).

37. *See, e.g.,* Brooms v. Regal Tube Co., 881 F.2d 412 (7th Cir. 1989).

38. Wheeler v. Southland Corp., 875 F.2d 1246 (6th Cir. 1989). *See also* Watts v. New York City Police Dep't, 724 F. Supp. 99 (S.D.N.Y. 1991) (unexecuted threats made to probationary employee).

39. Burns v. McGregor Elec. Indus., Inc., 1992 U.S. Dist LEXIS (N.D. Iowa, April 7, 1992) (upon reversal and remand by the Eighth District Court of Appeals on January 30, 1992).

to watch pornographic movies, and improperly touched her on at least two occasions. The court found that the alleged victim was not, however, "at least as affected as the reasonable person in like circumstances" based upon her personal history, "her manner of dress, her pierced, bejeweled nipples, the location of her tattoo [on her pelvic region]," the fact that she had appeared nude more than once "in a magazine [Easy Rider] containing much lewd and crude sexually explicit material, and her appearance on the stand that the type of conduct in which [her employer] engaged was not in and of itself offensive to her."[40] In sum, the court found that even though the sexual harassment would be actionable by a reasonable person, it was not actionable by the alleged victim because she was not a "reasonable" person.

C. Employer Liability for *Quid Pro Quo* and Hostile Environment Harassment of an Employee by Her Supervisor

1. *Quid Pro Quo* Liability

In *quid pro quo* harassment cases, an employer is generally strictly liable for conduct of supervisory employees who have complete authority over hiring, advancement, dismissal and discipline of employees under the theory of *respondeat superior*.[41] The Supreme Court has implicitly endorsed this position when it stated "where a supervisor exercises the authority actually delegated to him by his employer, by making or threatening to make decisions affecting the employment status of his subordinates, such actions are properly imputed to the employer whose delegation of authority empowered the supervisor to undertake them."[42] The rationale and theory behind strict liability is that the supervisor's extortion of sexual favors is a *quid pro quo* for job benefits which he has the power to bestow as furnished to him by the employer. Where a supervisor uses the means, authority or power furnished to him by his employer to accomplish

---

40. *Id.*

41. EEOC Guidelines. Highlander v. K.F.C. Nat'l Management Co., 805 F.2d 644, 648 (6th Cir. 1986). *Accord* Chamberlain v. 101 Realty, Inc., 915 F.2d 777 (1st Cir. 1990); Sparks v. Pilot Freight Carriers, Inc., 830 F.2d 1554 (11th Cir. 1987); Horn v. Duke Homes, 755 F.2d 599 (7th Cir. 1985); Craig v. Y & Y Snacks, Inc., 721 F.2d 77 (3d Cir. 1983); Henson v. City of Dundee, 682 F.2d 897 (11th Cir. 1982); Miller v. Bank of Am., 600 F.2d 211 (9th Cir. 1979); Barnes v. Costle, 561 F.2d 983 (D.C. Cir. 1977).

42. Meritor Sav. Bank v. Vinson, 477 U.S. 57, 70 (1986).

his prohibited purpose, he acts within the scope of his actual or apparent authority to hire, fire, discipline or promote making the employer strictly liable.[43] Put another way, when a supervisory employee with absolute authority to hire and fire uses his authority to extort sexual favors from employees, he is the institution and, thus, the institution is held strictly liable.[44]

Where the supervisor lacks plenary or absolute authority, liability often may not be strictly imputed to the employer. For example, an employer is not liable where the employee who makes sexual advances against another lacks authority to terminate or effectively recommend termination of the employee.[45] However, liability may be imputed via "apparent authority" where the harassed employee reasonably believes the harasser possesses such authority. Liability may also be imputed to an employer via estoppel, if the employer carelessly or intentionally causes an employee to mistakenly believe the supervisor has plenary hiring authority on behalf of the employer. Liability may also be imputed where the employer is negligent or reckless in supervising the harasser, particularly where the employer knew or had constructive knowledge of the harassment but failed to act to stop it.[46]

Finally, liability may be imputed where the supervisor was aided in accomplishing the tort by the existence of an agency relationship. For example, where a supervisor intimates to an employee that he can fire her if she fails to comply with his advances, he accomplishes his prohibited acts by virtue of his agency relationship with the company.[47] The moral of the story is that even if an employee is not a supervisor with complete hiring authority, liability still may be imputed to an educational institution for *quid pro quo* harassment.

2. Hostile Environment Liability

In "hostile environment" cases, the courts and the EEOC are less eager to impose strict liability on employers. In the *Meritor* case, where hostile environment harassment was first recognized, the

---

43. Steele v. Offshore Shipbuilding, Inc., 867 F.2d 1311, 1316 (11th Cir. 1989).

44. Horn v. Duke Homes, 755 F.2d 599 (7th Cir.1985); Carrero v. New York City Hous. Auth., 890 F.2d 569, 579 (2d Cir. 1989) ("in *quid pro quo* cases the harassing employee acts as and for the company, holding out the employer's benefits as an inducement to the employee for sexual favors. Accordingly, in a *quid pro quo* sexual harassment case, the employer is held strictly liable for its employee's unlawful acts").

45. Fisher v. Flynn, 598 F.2d 663 (1st Cir. 1979).

46. Hicks v. Gates Rubber Co., 833 F.2d 1406, 1418 (10th Cir. 1987); Fields v. Horizon House, Inc., Case No. 86-4343 (E.D. Pa., Dec. 9, 1987).

47. Sparks v. Pilot Freight Carriers, Inc., 830 F.2d 1554 (11th Cir. 1987).

Supreme Court declined to issue a definitive rule on employer liability, merely noting courts should look to agency principles for guidance.[48] In *Meritor*, the Court held that an employer's policy against discrimination and the existence of a grievance procedure were relevant to the issue of liability, but did not necessarily insulate the employer.[49]

Since the Supreme Court spoke in *Meritor*, the EEOC has maintained that an employer is liable when a supervisor creates a hostile work environment and the employer knew or had reason to know of the misconduct and failed to take prompt remedial action:

> The commission generally will find an employer liable for "hostile environment" sexual harassment by a supervisor when the employer failed to establish an explicit policy against sexual harassment and did not have a reasonably available avenue by which victims of sexual harassment could complain to someone with authority to investigate and remedy the problem. . . . But an employer can divest its superiors of this apparent authority by implementing a strong policy against sexual harassment and maintaining an effective complaint procedure. When employees know that recourse is available, they cannot reasonably believe that a harassing work environment is authorized or condoned by an employer.[50]

Knowledge, actual or constructive, can be imputed to the employer from first-hand observation, internal complaints, the pervasiveness of the harassment, or the employer's indifference to sexual harassment, reflected by a failure to establish a policy and a grievance mechanism to redress it. Essentially, an employer's failure to remedy or prevent a hostile environment where it knew, or reasonably should have known, will create a basis for liability for the sexual harassment of its employees.

Educational institutions must be warned that the absence of its actual or constructive notice does not necessarily insulate it from liability. As in *quid pro quo* cases, liability will be imputed to the institu-

---

49. *Id.*

50. *EEOC Guidance Memorandum to Field Personnel*, 57 L.W. 2261 (Oct. 17, 1988). *See* Henson v. City of Dundee, 682 F.2d 897, 905 (11th Cir. 1982); Hirschfeld v. New Mexico Corrections Dep't, 916 F.2d 572 (10th Cir. 1990); Steele v. Offshore Shipbuilding, Inc., 876 F.2d 1311 (11th Cir. 1989); Yates v. AVCO Corp., 819 F.2d 630 (6th Cir. 1987); RESTATEMENT SECOND AGENCY § 219(2)(b) (1958).

tion where it is aware or should have been aware of a supervisor's sexually harassing conduct, and does nothing to remedy the situation.[51]

D. The Tough Case of Equals Versus Equals: Educational Institution Liability for *Quid Pro Quo* and Hostile Environment Sexual Harassment of Co-Workers

Harassment between co-workers generally does not subject an institution to strict liability because co-workers are not normally in a situation to influence or alter the victim's employment status.[52] In short, neither employee has bargaining leverage. However, where an institution knows or should have known of co-worker harassment but fails to take reasonable and prompt remedial action, it may be held to have authorized or ratified the action and liability may be imputed.[53]

E. Sexual Harassment as a Violation of 42 U.S.C. Section 1983 and Equal Protection

1. 42 U.S.C. Section 1983

An employee may bring suit under federal statute, 42 U.S.C. section 1983, against a public educational institution and individuals for alleged violation of the Constitution or federal law while acting "under color of state law."[54] In order to establish liability under 42 U.S.C. section 1983, a plaintiff must prove that the public educational institution itself supported the alleged violation of the victim's rights. In particular, harassment must result from a custom, pattern of behavior or policy of the governing body.[55]

---

51. EEOC v. Gurnee Inn Corp., 914 F.2d 817 (7th Cir. 1990); EEOC v. Hacienda Hotel, 881 F.2d 1504 (9th Cir. 1989).

52. *See* Weinsheimer v. Rockwell Int'l Corp., 754 F. Supp. 1559 (M.D. Fla. 1990), *aff'd*, 949 F.2d 1162 (11th Cir. 1991).

53. 29 C.F.R. 1604.11(d).

54. 42 U.S.C. § 1983 states:

> Every person who, under color of any statute, ordinance, regulation, custom, or usage, of any State or Territory or the District of Columbia, subjects, or causes to be subjected, any citizen of the United States or other person within the jurisdiction thereof to the deprivation of any rights, privileges, or immunities secured by the Constitution and laws, shall be liable to the party injured in an action at law, suit in equity, or other proper proceeding for redress.

55. *See* Carrero v. New York City Hous. Auth., 890 F.2d 569 (2d Cir. 1989).

For example, in *Bohen v. City of E. Chicago, Ind.*,[56] the court concluded that a dispatcher, who was subjected to repeated harassment including sexual touching, lurid sexual remarks and threats of rape, had an actionable claim under 42 U.S.C. section 1983 as well as under the equal protection clause which is discussed in the following section. Not only were women intentionally discriminated against by the fire department and the city, but supervisory personnel and management officials either were aware of, participated in, or accepted the practice of sexual harassment within the department. Thus, in sum, the court found the harassment resulted from a custom and practice of the governing body in violation of section 1983.

The courts are not clear whether a public institution must consider a sexual harassment policy or harassing behavior and explicitly reject it or refuse to act, or whether mere failure to act is sufficient to form a custom or policy of endorsing sexual harassment. One thing is crystal clear, however, a viable sexual harassment policy which provides reporting and investigation procedures goes a long way to dispel such institutional liability.

Under section 1983, an alleged victim may also state a claim against an institution for the harassing acts of a supervisor where the supervisor has been delegated complete policy-making authority. The theory is that a public educational institution delegates such authority to a supervisor who then has all authority to create a custom or policy which may be imputed to the institution.

A public educational institution, however, will not be liable simply because it gives a supervisor discretion regarding employment decisions. Moreover, a public employer's mere failure to investigate a supervisor's discretionary decisions does not amount to a delegation of policy-making authority. Once again, if a public educational institution has an effective policy prohibition *explicitly against* sexual harassment, a supervisor's actions will be more difficult to impute to the employer.[57]

The plaintiff must show a custom or policy of harassment by one with policy making authority. In one case, a group of female police officers were referred to in an offensive and obscene manner, pornographic pictures of women were displayed and personal property was

---

56. 799 F.2d 1180 (7th Cir. 1986).

57. In *Carrero*, the supervisor's actions could not be attributed to the Housing Authority because the Housing Authority's policies were explicitly non-discriminatory. Although the supervisor was given discretion in training and evaluating the plaintiff employee, "discretion in the exercise of particular functions does not, without more, give rise to municipal liability based on an exercise of that discretion." *Carrero*, 890 F.2d at 577 (quoting Pembaur v. City of Cincinnati, 475 U.S. 469, 482 (1986)).

stolen and vandalized.[58] The City was found not to have a custom or policy for sexual harassment where the Police Commissioner, the plenary policy maker, had promulgated and disseminated a police department training manual explaining the prohibitions against sexual harassment and discrimination.[59] In addition, bulletins and regulations were issued outlining the duties of police officers with respect to the department's anti-discrimination policy. The Commissioner also established an Equal Employment Office to review discrimination claims. Since the Police Commissioner, the plenary policy maker, did not authorize or acquiesce in the sexual harassment, the court found the City could not be held liable for discrimination under section 1983.

The same court found, however, that the supervisor involved in the case acquiesced in the sexual harassment of female officers and was aware of problems but did nothing to stop them. The supervisor also failed to make any investigation of the claims brought by the women. Thus, the supervisor was liable for harassment under section 1983, but his acquiescence was not imputed to the City because he lacked plenary, policy-making authority.[60]

2. Equal Protection

An employee may also sue a public educational institution for violation of equal protection under the Constitution. To do so, the employee must allege that sexual harassment is *intentional*.[61] The *intent* of the harasser is a key element under equal protection claims. By contrast, the inquiry under Title VII is based on the alleged *victim's perspective* of the harassment.[62] If an employee can demonstrate intentional sexual harassment, the equal protection claim will be actionable under 42 U.S.C. section 1983, giving rise to compensatory and punitive damages.

The conscious failure of the employer to protect an employee from the abusive conditions created by fellow employees may support an equal protection action. However, the employer may defend itself by showing "the harassment suffered by the plaintiff was directed at [her] because of factors personal to her and not because she is a

---

58. Andrews v. City of Philadelphia, 895 F.2d 1469 (3d Cir. 1990).

59. *Id.*

60. *Id.* at 1478.

61. Bohen v. City of E. Chicago, Ind., 799 F.2d 1180 (7th Cir. 1986).

62. King v. Board of Regents of Univ. of Wis. Sys., 898 F.2d 533, 537-38 (7th Cir. 1990).

woman."[63] In such a case, the poor treatment is based on the fact that, for example, others do not like a particular employee, regardless of her sex.

F. State Common Law Torts and Other Sources of Recovery

The same facts which give rise to a claim for discrimination under state and federal statutes may also give rise to various state common law tort claims including intentional and negligent infliction of emotional distress, assault and battery, and invasion of privacy. The law in some states, however, precludes common law recoveries for sexual harassment and limits an employee to discrimination statutes.[64]

In addition, some states have found the state workers' compensation statute does not provide the exclusive remedy for sexual harassment in the workplace nor are such claims barred by workers' compensation immunity or subject to privileges accorded in an intentional tort statute.[65] Once again, however, other states have found employees are limited to suit under the state workers' compensation statute.[66]

G. Romance and Harassment

Even fuzzier lines appear as to definitions of actionable sexual harassment when it comes to romance or favoritism between employees. As women and men now work together in all aspects of the workplace, issues of romance and favoritism have been raised and continue to perplex institutions. What is the role of the employer when romance goes sour, becomes or begins one-sided, and creates an intolerable working environment? What about when a person is pro-

---

63. Bohen v. City of E. Chicago, Ind., 799 F.2d 1180, 1187 (7th Cir. 1986).

64. *See, e.g.*, Irvin Investors, Inc. v. Superior Court, 166 Ariz. 113, 800 P.2d 979 (1991); Guess v. Bethlehem Steel Corp., 913 F.2d 463 (7th Cir.1990); Davis v. Utah Power & Light, 53 F.E.P. Cases 1331 (D. Utah 1990); Haddon v. Metropolitan Life Ins. Co., 52 F.E.P. Cases 478 (Va. Sup. Ct. 1990).

65. *See, e.g.*, Kerans v. Porter Paint Co., 61 Ohio St. 3d 486, 493, 575 N.E.2d 428 (1991); Byrd v. Richardson-Greenshields Sec., Inc., 552 So. 2d 1099 (Fla. Sup. Ct. 1989) (holding workers' compensation statute not the exclusive vehicle for claims of assault and battery, intentional infliction of emotional distress, negligent hiring and retention of employees by women employees claiming emotional stress caused by offensive touching and sexual advances).

66. *See, e.g.*, Crofts v. Harrison, 772 S.W.2d 901, 50 F.E.P. Cases 515 (Mo. Ct. App. 1989); Knox v. Combined Ins. Co., 50 F.E.P. Cases 568 (Me. Sup. Jud. 1988) (injuries arising out of employment are subject to exclusive workers compensation statute); Studstill v. Borg Warner Acceptance Corp., 806 F.2d 1005 (11th Cir. 1986).

moted by a supervisor who hopes he will receive romance or sexual attention?

In February 1990, the EEOC issued its *Policy Guidance on Employer Liability for Sexual Favoritism* which establishes three basic principles relating to these questions but provides little substantive assistance. First, the EEOC suggests isolated instances of favoritism towards a "paramour" are not prohibited. According to the EEOC, an isolated instance of favoritism toward a lover, a spouse or a friend may be unfair, but it does not discriminate against women or men in violation of Title VII, since "both are disadvantaged for reasons other than their genders."[67]

Second, favoritism based upon coerced sexual conduct may constitute *quid pro quo* harassment. Where a female employee is coerced into submitting to unwelcome sexual advances in return for a job benefit, other female employees who were qualified for, but denied, the benefit may sue under Title VII on the theory that sex was generally made a condition for receiving the benefit. This may well be true even though the woman who was granted preferential treatment was engaged in a consensual affair with her supervisor, in the face of evidence that the supervisor made telephone calls to proposition several female employees at home and at the office.[68] On the other hand, an employee who chooses to become involved in an intimate affair with her employer cannot be heard to complain of harassment when he reacts emotionally to her decision to end the relationship.[69] In this vein, sexual activity premised on personal attraction is not evidence of discriminatory intent.[70]

Finally, the EEOC intimated that widespread favoritism may constitute hostile environment harassment. If favoritism based upon the granting of sexual favors is widespread in a workplace, both male and female colleagues who do not welcome this conduct can establish a hostile work environment in violation of Title VII, regardless of whether those who were granted favorable treatment willingly bestowed the sexual favors. The EEOC reasons that under these circumstances, a message is conveyed that the managers view women as "sexual playthings," thereby creating an atmosphere that is demeaning to women. Both men and women who find this environment

---

67. *Accord* Miller v. Aluminum Co. of Am., 679 F. Supp. 495 (W.D. Pa), *aff'd mem.*, 856 F.2d 184 (3d Cir. 1988). *But see* King v. Palmer, 778 F.2d 878 (D.C. Cir. 1985).

68. *See, e.g.*, Toscano v. Nimmo, 570 F. Supp. 1197, 1199-1201 (D. Del. 1983).

69. Keppler v. Hinsdale Township High Sch. Dist. 86, 715 F. Supp. 862 (N.D. Ill. 1989). *But see* Babcock v. Frank, 729 F. Supp. 279 (S.D.N.Y. 1991).

70. Trautvetter v. Quick, 916 F.2d 1140 (7th Cir. 1991).

offensive can establish a violation if the conduct is sufficiently severe or pervasive to alter the conditions of their employment and create an abusive working environment.[71]

VI. SEXUAL HARASSMENT OF STUDENTS

Educators are often unaware of sexual harassment of students in their institutions until they have been involved in a sex discrimination lawsuit or attended a discrimination workshop.[72] The tendency of educators to ignore, downplay or be unaware of sexual harassment may well be due to their failure to recognize particular behavior as sexual harassment. Research shows behavior which qualifies as harassment is often not recognized as such by the harasser or the harassee.[73] Moreover, some educators ignore harassment due to a lack of desire to become involved, particularly when there previously has been no penalty for doing so.

Over the last year, educational institutions have had a rude awakening regarding sexual harassment of students. The first message was delivered by the Supreme Court, which ruled that monetary damages are available to students for violations of Title IX of the Education Amendments of 1972.[74] This has been followed by several lawsuits and administrative charges brought by students against school districts for sexual harassment by other students which have settled out of court for tens of thousands of dollars. The uncontroverted implication from these later cases is that school districts may have liability to their students for sexual harassment by other students, otherwise known as peer harassment.[75] In the future, more suits may be brought and actually litigated against educational institutions for peer harassment.

The overall message is clear — those educators who were not previously persuaded to pay attention to sexual harassment and peer

---

71. *See, e.g.*, Broderick v. Ruder, 685 F. Supp. 1269 (D.D.C. 1988).

72. The AAUW Report, HOW SCHOOLS SHORTCHANGE GIRLS, (1992), at 8 [hereinafter HOW SCHOOLS SHORTCHANGE GIRLS].

73. Pauldi and Barickman, ACADEMIC AND WORKPLACE SEXUAL HARASSMENT, at 67 (1991).

74. Franklin v. Gwinnett County Pub. Schools, 112 S. Ct. 1028 (1992)

75. Peer harassment has been recognized on college campuses for years. *See, e.g.*, Hughes, PEER HARASSMENT HASSLES FOR WOMEN ON CAMPUS (1988).

harassment in their institutions are now forced to do so as a result of the threat of potential litigation and the tug at purse strings. With potential exposure to hefty damages, not to mention attorneys fees, educational institutions must take a pro-active stance and confront the issue of sexual harassment.

This section describes sexual harassment of students by employees of the institution as well as by other students. It favors an affirmative approach which includes establishing a policy against sexual harassment as well as a reporting and complaint procedure. The plan also incorporates educating the institution's populace about sexual harassment through the school newspaper, the use of questionnaires, and the like. Also included are suggestions for modifying student conduct codes and disciplinary policies.

A. Background: Students Have a Cause of Action Against Institutions That Receive Federal Funds for Sexual Harassment Under Title IX of the Education Amendments of 1972

Over a decade ago, the Supreme Court recognized a student's implied right of action for discrimination under Title IX of the Education Amendments of 1972.[76] Title IX bars discrimination in educational programs that receive federal funds:

> No person in the United States shall, on the basis of sex, be excluded from participation in, be denied the benefits of, or be subjected to discrimination under any education program or activity receiving Federal financial assistance.[77]

Discrimination under Title IX includes sexual harassment which has been defined by the Office of Civil Rights of the United States Department of Education as:

> Verbal or physical conduct of a sexual nature, imposed on the basis of sex, by an employee or agent of a recipient that denies, limits, provides different, or conditions the provision of aid, benefits, services or treatment protected under Title IX.

Researchers have gone one step further to define sexual harassment empirically on a continuum, ranging from gender harassment to

---

76. Cannon v. University of Chicago, 441 U.S. 677 (1979).
77. 20 U.S.C. § 1681(a).

sexual assault. For example, one researcher defines sexual harassing behavior as (1) gender harassment including "generalized sexist statements and behavior that convey insulting, degrading, and/or sexist attitudes"; (2) seductive behavior including "unwanted, inappropriate, and offensive physical or verbal sexual advances"; (3) sexual bribery including "solicitation of sexual activity or other sex-linked behavior by promise of reward"; (4) sexual coercion includes "coercion or sexual activity or other sex-linked behavior by threat of punishment"; and (5) sexual assault includes "assault and/or rape."[78]

Indeed, part of the controversy revolving around sexual harassment is the inability to identify it. As will be described in more detail below, sexual harassment comes in many shapes and sizes and, oftentimes, is behavior which has been formerly accepted and viewed as innocuous by the general population.

B. Damages Are Available for Violations of Title IX of the Education Amendments of 1972

Historically, Title IX was thought to provide only injunctive relief to stop discriminatory practices, allowing only "equitable" relief to make the victim whole (e.g., back pay). Recognizing that this relief is inadequate in many cases, the Supreme Court determined monetary damages are also available for violations of Title IX. In *Franklin v. Gwinnett County Public Schools*,[79] the Supreme Court unanimously held a female student could maintain a damage action for sexual harassment and abuse against a Georgia school district and a former administrator under Title IX. The Court concluded back pay would not apply to the student and injunctive relief was ineffective because the student no longer attended the school.[80] *Gwinnett*[81] involves a staggering demand of *$6 million* in damages from the school district and the administrator. The determination of damages (if the case does not settle first) has yet to be made by the trier of fact.

---

78. Pauldi and Barickman, ACADEMIC AND WORKPLACE SEXUAL HARASSMENT, at 6 (1991).

79. 112 S. Ct. 1028 (1992).

80. The student in *Gwinnett* filed a complaint with the Office of Civil Rights of the United States Department of Education. The OCR investigated the charges and concluded the district had violated the student's rights by subjecting her to sexual harassment an interfering with her right to complain about it. The OCR found, however, the district had come into compliance with Title IX because the teacher and an administrator had resigned, and the district had implemented a grievance procedure.

81. 112 S. Ct. 1028 (1992).

C. The Easy Case of Unequals: Educational Institution Liability for Sexual Harassment of Its Students by Its Employees

Gwinnett[82] involved sexual harassment by a teacher that allegedly occurred over a period of years. The harassment included sexually-oriented conversations, forcibly kissing the student, telephone calls and coerced intercourse in the teacher's office. The student additionally alleged the district was aware of and investigated her allegations of sexual harassment and abuse, but no action was taken to put a stop to it and she was discouraged from pressing charges. Furthermore, the district did not have a formal policy and procedure for reporting and investigation of sexual harassment and abuse. Ultimately, the teacher was fired and the district implemented a policy and procedure to deal with harassment. However, it was too little, too late.

In a recent Illinois case, Northwestern University took a hit when one of its professor's embarked in a classic case of *quid pro quo* harassment of a doctoral student. Judge Berman wrote that "courts will ordinarily defer to the discretion of school officials and rarely review an educational institution's evaluation of the academic performance of its students. However, when a court finds an educational institution's actions to be arbitrary, capricious or motivated by bad faith, judicial intervention is warranted."[83]

D. The Toughest Case: Educational Institution Liability for Peer Harassment

The newest bastion for sexual harassment violations under Title IX exists in the area of institutional liability for sexual harassment of students *by other students*, otherwise known as peer harassment. Actionable peer harassment may include harassment in its more identifiable forms including physical abuse. However, it may also include behavior which has been formerly viewed as innocuous. A recent report by the American Association of University Women sets the stage for institutional liability based upon the "boys will be boys" perception of peer harassment:

---

82. *Id.*

83. Fegelman, *Professor, NU Are Rebuked in Student's Suit*, Chicago Tribune, Dec. 17, 1992, Chicagoland Section, at 22, col. 1.

> There is mounting evidence that boys do not treat girls well. Reports of student sexual harassment—the unwelcome verbal or physical conduct of a sexual nature imposed by one individual on another—among junior high school and high school peers are increasing. In the majority of cases a boy is harassing a girl. . . .
>
> Sexual harassment is prohibited under Title IX, yet sex-biased peer interactions appear to be permitted in schools, if not always approved. Rather than viewing sexual harassment as a serious misconduct, school authorities too often treat it as a joke.
>
> When boys line up to "rate" girls as they enter a room, when boys treat girls so badly that they are reluctant to enroll in courses where they may be the only female, when boys feel it is good fun to embarrass girls to the point of tears, it is no joke. Yet these types of behaviors are often viewed by school personnel as harmless instances of "boys being boys". . . .
>
> When schools ignore sexist, racist, homophobic, and violent interactions between students, they are giving tacit approval to such behaviors. . . .[84]

There are ethical or moral reasons for burdening educational institutions with responsibility for sexual harassment of its students by other students. The most far-reaching of these are chicken and egg propositions: Do institutions merely reflect societal problems or are societal problems caused by behavior learned in educational institutions? One fact is clear — female students show residual signs of wear and tear as a result of their male counterparts' harassment throughout the years. The vast disparity between men and women in the work force makes it obvious that the underpinnings of sexual harassment begins well before entry into the workforce.[85]

Recognizing that school teaches youngsters social skills, as well as academic, it makes sense to sensitize students early on through education, policies, and disciplinary action. A pro-active approach will not only educate boys and young men, but will also educate and empower young women. Researchers have found that after the age of 12, girls are less likely to speak up and are more likely to tolerate harassment

---

84. How Schools Shortchange Girls, *supra* note 72, at 73-74.
85. How Schools Shortchange Girls, *supra* note 72, at 4-5.

because of repercussions and retaliation.[86] Moreover, unchecked harassment will surely continue.

1. A "Boys will be Boys" Response May Be Costly

Educational institutions may be liable to their students for sexual harassment by other students. Actionable behavior may include that which was formerly viewed as innocuous "boys will be boys" behavior. Over the last year, several school districts around the country have paid settlements to students who filed lawsuits or administrative charges for sexual harassment by other students.[87]

For example, a student sued the Petaluma School District in Northern San Francisco, along with her principal, for unchecked peer harassment. The student claimed when she was in the eighth grade, boys repeatedly mocked her before, during and after school, in the halls and on the bus.[88] They yelled "moo moo" and made vulgar references to her breasts and other parts of her anatomy.[89] The suit was settled when the school district paid the student $20,000.[90]

In Minnesota, a student received a $15,000 settlement for "mental anguish" after charging the Duluth Central High School with sexual harassment for failing to remove graffiti about her that was on the wall of a boys' bathroom. The graffiti called her a "slut" and made other sexual comments.[91]

Another Minnesota student attending Chaska High School was told that her name appeared on a list entitled the "25 most fuckable girls" in her class.[92]

She received an "honorable mention". After requesting school officials to conduct an investigation, she was told to drop the issue.[93] This student won her case, however, still pending is the question of compensation.[94]

Perhaps even more alarming are the number of sexual harassment cases arising from student behavior at the elementary level. Recently,

---

86. *Id.*

87. No doubt these settlements may have been promoted by insurance carriers of the schools. Nevertheless, the implication of potential liability is very real.

88. Ellicott, *Schools Outlaw Sexist Jokers*, The Times, Feb. 28, 1992, Modern Times, Life & Times Section, at 6.

89. *Id.*

90. *Id.*

91. *Id.*

92. *Id.*

93. *Id.*

94. Leighty, *When Teasing Goes Over The Line*, The San Francisco Chronicle, Nov. 8, 1992, § TW, at 12/Z1.

the mother of Cheltzie Hentz, a seven-year-old second-grader, in Eden Prairie, Minnesota, filed state and federal charges against her school district relating to sexual harassment of her daughter.[95] Cheltzie claims boys on the school bus used naughty language and teased her.[96] Specifically, the boys allegedly repeatedly used profanity, called her obscene names, referred to her genitalia and suggested Cheltzie perform oral sex on her father.[97] Cheltzie's mother complained verbally and in writing repeatedly to school officials. In response, the school disciplined the two boys and later removed them from the bus, providing them with alternative transportation.[98] School officials also spoke with the rest of the children regarding appropriate language on the bus, but the charges remain pending.[99]

In Illinois, a third-grade elementary student filed suit in court against a school district for its negligence allowing a fellow student to pinch her chest, groin and buttocks on several occasions during the first through third grades.[100] The boy also showed the girl a condom and talked about sex. The girl subsequently enrolled in private school and receives counseling regarding the incidents. The parents are now seeking compensation for private school tuition and the costs of the child's counseling.[101]

Finally, in a Northern California school, kindergarten girls complained about "flip-up Friday" when the boys would flip up their skirts and dresses at recess.[102] A teacher informed the parents of the children who put a stop to the behavior before suit could be filed.[103]

In sum, the number of cases alleging sexual harassment between peers in school is on the rise for a variety of allegedly actionable behaviors. Educational institutions can expect legal standards to be tested and refined with time, but at the present time, as is demonstrated by the foregoing examples, there appear to be few answers to educators most burning questions in this regard.

---

95. Will, *Our Expanding Menu of Rights*, NEWSWEEK, Dec. 14, 1992, at 90.

96. Hillbery, *Taunts on the School Bus Spark Girl's Sexual Harassment Complaint*, L.A. Times, Dec. 1, 1992, at 5, pt. A, col. 1.

97. Matheny, *Girl's Sexual-Harassment Charge has Experts Taking Closer Look At Kids' Behavior*, Minneapolis Star Tribune, Nov. 12, 1992, Variety Section, at 1E.

98. Gleick, *The Boys On The Bus*, PEOPLE MAGAZINE, Nov. 30, 1992, at 125.

99. Hillbery, *Taunts on the School Bus Spark Girl's Sexual Harassment Complaint*, L.A. Times, Dec. 1, 1992, at 5, pt. A, col. 1.

100. Kendall, *Sexual Harassment: Can It Happen In 3rd Grade?*, Chicago Tribune, Nov. 3, 1992, News Section, at 1, col. 1.

101. *Id.*

102. Leighty, *When Teasing Goes Over The Line*, The San Francisco Chron., Nov. 8, 1992, § TW, at 12/Z1.

103. *Id.*

2. Identifying Actionable Behavior by Peers

What student behavior might be actionable and create institutional liability? It is impossible to prepare a list of all behavior which might constitute sexual harassment in classrooms, hallways, on playgrounds, buses, or the athletic field. Verbal and physical abuse and harassment such as snapping a bra strap, poking a girl in the breast, sexual jokes, sexual graffiti, stereotypical portrayals of women in school skits, rating of girls, and cat calls likely constitute sexual harassment which, unchecked, could create institutional liability. At present, educators should err on the conservative side, promptly investigate complaints and sincerely enforce any policies via appropriate warnings and discipline.

As a general rule of thumb, regardless of its source, when harassment is based on the victim's sex, it may be sexual harassment. If educational institutions are liable for sexual harassment of its girl students by boys, the reverse is also true. While it may be less common, girls are not immune from harassing boys both physically and verbally potentially creating liability to the educational institution. Moreover, harassment related to sexual orientation or sexual preference may also be actionable.[104]

Query though how far institutions will get drawn into legislating and regulating student behavior and relationships. For example, what is the role of the institution in regard to student dating and romance? What is the role of the institution when romance goes bad? What should institutions do about dances and other social functions, making out in the halls, and students' suggestive dress?

E. The Duty To Protect and Provide a Safe Educational Environment

The controversy over whether an educational institution's affirmative duty to protect its students from sexual harassment is not new. Students have attempted to establish such a right primarily by suing school districts and their employees under a federal civil rights statute, 42 U.S.C. section 1983.[105] Similar to an employee, a student may, under section 1983, sue an educational institution and its

---

104. HOW SCHOOLS SHORTCHANGE GIRLS, *supra* note 72, at 73-74.

105. The school district, Board and supervisors are liable for violative actions of an employee only where the employee's conduct was caused by official policy or custom attributable to the superior official or district. *See* Monell v. Department of Social Servs., 436 U.S. 658 (1978).

employees for monetary damages and, declaratory or injunctive relief for deprivations of constitutional or federal rights when such is done under "color of state law."

Generally speaking, in order to state a claim under 42 U.S.C. section 1983, a student must allege she possesses a constitutionally protected right or some federal right of which she has been deprived as a result of an official policy or custom of the educational institution. Students have attempted to establish claims under section 1983 through the use of two theories. The first theory arises from an alleged special relationship between the institution and the student in its "custody." The second theory arises from an alleged persistent pattern of deliberate indifference.

1. Custodial Relationship

The first theory entails the allegation of a special relationship between the institution and the student which imposes affirmative duties of care and protection upon the institution with respect to its students' health, safety and welfare. This duty allegedly arises out of a special custodial relationship created by truancy laws which has been likened to children held in foster care and prisoners held by their jailers. In most cases, this theory has been rejected by the courts primarily because parental authority extends to students while they are in school which ameliorates the so-called special relationship.

In 1989, the Supreme Court specifically visited and rejected the special relationship issue in *DeShaney v. Winnebago County Department of Social Services.*[106] The Court found there was no affirmative duty to protect a child where a child is *not in state custody* and where the actions were taken by a private individual. In reliance on *DeShaney*, many courts have similarly rejected the special relationship theory.[107]

---

106. 489 S. Ct. 189 (1989).

107. *See, e.g.*, Elliott v. New Miami Bd. of Educ., 799 F. Supp. 818, 823 (S.D. Ohio 1992) (rejecting special relationship because parents are the primary caretakers of student, while admitting the school's relationship with its students is "unique"); Doe v. Douglas County Sch. Dist., 770 F. Supp. 591 (D. Colo. 1991) (rejected the special relationship argument in the school setting for a child alleging molestation by a school psychologist because compulsory attendance does not make a child unable to care for basic human needs. Parents retain primary responsibility for feeding, clothing, shelter, and caring); J.O. v. Alton Community Sch., 909 F.2d 267, 272 (7th Cir. 1990) (compulsory attendance laws do not put a special duty to protect when a child dies during gym class). *But see* Pagano v. Massapequa Pub. Schs., 714 F. Supp. 641 (E.D.N.Y. 1989) (refusing to dismiss cause of action finding elementary school students who are required to attend school must be owed some duty of care; student alleged seventeen incidents of physical and verbal abuse of which the district and administrators were aware and failed to prevent).

For example, in *Dorothy J. v. District*,[108] a federal court found a student who was raped by a fellow student could not bring a claim under section 1983 against district officials. The boy was sexually molested and raped while attending a special program for mentally-handicapped students at the high school. The student's parent alleged the school district knew of the violent propensity of the attacker and deprived the student of his Fourteenth Amendment rights. The court held the school officials had no duty to protect the child from attack.

On the other hand, in somewhat of a landmark decision, *Doe v. Taylor Independent School District*,[109] the Fifth Circuit recognized the existence of a special relationship arising from the state's requirement compelling a child to attend public school: "by compelling a child to attend public school, the state cultivates a special relationship with that child and thus owes him an affirmative duty of protection." In *Doe v. Taylor Independent School District*,[110] the student alleged a long-term pattern of behavior by her teacher including his writing several love letters and eventually resulting in her repeated seduction and performance of sex and oral sex. This case has been remanded for trial under the special relationship standard enunciated by the Fifth Circuit.

2. Educational Institution Will Be Responsible Where Student Establishes the Educational Institution's Custom or Policy of Deliberate Indifference

The second theory of recovery presented by students is the educational institution's deliberate or reckless indifference to the sexually harassing behavior. In *Stoneking v. Bradford Area School District*,[111] a school band director allegedly used physical force, threats of reprisal, intimidation and coercion to sexually abuse and harass female student into engaging in sexual acts. The student brought suit against district and alleged school authorities were aware of the employee's misconduct and failed to take action to protect the student's health, safety and welfare. Since the school district had been put on notice of the allegations and had taken no action or had discouraged complaints by students, the schools actions or inactions constituted an official custom and practice of reckless or deliberate indifference.

---

108. LR-C-91-801 (E.D. Ark. May 28, 1992).
109. 975 F.2d 137 (5th Cir. 1992) (remanded for trial).
110. *Id.*
111. 856 F.2d 594 (3d Cir. 1988), *reh. denied*, 882 F.2d 720 (1989).

The proof necessary to establish an official custom and practice of reckless or deliberate indifference to sexual harassment is fairly onerous. Claims of deliberate indifference have been rejected where complaints that a bus driver kissed a boy and used foul language were ignored by the school.[112] Five complaints of sexual abuse over a period of 16 years has been determined not to be a persistent, widespread pattern of ignoring complaints, particularly where a school had a child abuse training program.[113]

Most recently, the issue of whether public schools have a constitutional duty to protect students from harm during school hours has been submitted to the Supreme Court who has yet to decide whether it will review the case.[114] In *Middle Bucks*,[115] two high school girls were sexually assaulted by a group of teenage boys several times a week for a period of five months in a unisex bathroom and in a photographic darkroom at the school.[116] The most egregious acts of the assaults included that the girls' breasts and genitalia were touched, they were sodomized, forced to touch the boys genitalia and perform acts of fellatio. The court found there was insufficient notice to school officials to support a policy of reckless indifference necessary to find liability. *Middle Bucks*[117] is one of few court decisions to address the school's duty to protect students from student behavior as opposed to teacher behavior. On this same issue in *Elliott*, a federal district court recently held that students are private actors and, thus, there is no institutional liability because they do not act under color of state law.[118]

On the other hand, in *Doe v. Taylor Independent School District*,[119] the Fifth Circuit recently found a freshman high school student had a constitutional right under the due process and equal protection claus-

---

112. Jane Doe v. Special Sch. Dist. of St. Louis County, 901 F.2d 642 (8th Cir. 1990) (ignoring many complaints that a bus driver kissed a boy and used foul language did not amount to a continuing, widespread and persistent pattern of unconstitutional misconduct by employees, deliberate indifference or tacit authorization so as to amount to a custom and practice of ignoring complaints of physical and sexual abuse. Later, the bus driver pled guilty to child abuse of five children).

113. Thelma by Delores A. v. Board of Educ., 934 F.2d 926 (8th Cir. 1991).

114. D.R. v. Middle Bucks Area Vocational Technical School, 972 F.2d 1364 (3d Cir. 1992) (petition for certiorari filed November 9, 1992). The district court and a three-member appellate panel rejected the alleged duty because there was not enough evidence of notice to the school and, thus, not enough evidence of "reckless indifference." D.R. v. Middle Bucks Area Vocational Technical Sch., 1991 U.S. Dist. LEXIS 1292 (E.D. Pa. 1991), *aff'd*, 1991 U.S. App. LEXIS 30323 (3d Cir. 1991). An eleven-member panel reviewed the case *en banc* and affirmed judgment. 972 F.2d 1364 (3d Cir. 1992).

115. *Id.*

116. Several of the boys were pled guilty to or were convicted of criminal acts.

117. 972 F.2d 1364 (3d Cir. 1992).

118. Elliott v. New Miami Bd. of Educ., 799 F. Supp. 818 (S.D. Ohio 1992).

119. 975 F.2d 137 (5th Cir. 1992) (remanding for trial).

es of the Fourteenth Amendment to be free from sexual molestation by a state-employed school teacher. Moreover, the Court found that the superintendent and principal of the school had an affirmative duty to protect the student from such an intrusion.

The Court remanded for a trial after finding potential evidence that the superintendent and principal acted with deliberate indifference toward the student's constitutional rights. The test enunciated by the court included proof by the alleged student that (1) "school officials 'received notice of a pattern of unconstitutional acts committed by subordinates'"; (2) "school officials 'demonstrated deliberate indifference to or tacit authorization of the offensive acts'"; (3) "school officials 'failed to take sufficient remedial action'"; and (4) "such failure proximately caused injury to the student."

F. Educational Institutions May Be Liable on a Theory of Negligent Hiring or Retention of an Employee

A student may have a cause of action against an educational institution based upon the theory of negligent hiring or retention. The elements of a cause of action for negligent hiring include (1) the existence of an employment relationship; (2) an employee's incompetence or unfitness for the position; (3) the employer's actual or constructive knowledge of such incompetence or unfitness; (4) the employee's act or omission causing plaintiff's injury; and (5) the employer's negligent hiring or retention of the employee was the proximate cause of plaintiff's injuries.

Negligent hiring or retention scenarios may arise where an institution hires or retains an employee with knowledge that the employee has committed acts of sexual harassment or abuse, or other discrimination, and the employee "strikes again." The key question in such a case will focus on the institution's actual or constructive knowledge of the employee's behavior.

In the case of negligent hiring, the inquiry will look primarily to affirmative steps taken during the pre-employment investigation of a prospective employee and whether the investigation is adequate to extricate the district from liability for the teacher's misconduct.[120] The use of thorough pre-employment investigation procedures may prevent institutional liability down the road for sexual harassment, discrimination and other abuse. The best way to deal with such an inves-

---

120. *See, e.g.*, D.T. v. Independent Sch. Dist., 894 F.2d 1176 (10th Cir. 1990) (§ 1983 negligent hiring case); Smith v. Wickline, 396 F. Supp. 555 (W.D. Okla. 1975).

tigation is to establish a written policy which will provide a uniform procedure to be followed and also provide a checklist to make sure all bases are covered.

Applications and resumes should be carefully scrutinized as they may reveal more from what they do not state, than what they do state. For example, interviewees must be questioned about gaps in employment. References and past employers must be contacted. Responses of those contacted must be documented including refusals to divulge information on the basis of company policy or otherwise. Require applicants to sign a waiver releasing former employers from liability for disclosing information, personnel records and appraisals. If the applicant refuses to do so, ask why. Potential employers should seek affirmative attestations of the applicant's good character.

Many state laws now require or permit educational institutions to conduct criminal and child abuse record checks. Institutions should condition employment upon the results of these records checks. Teaching certificates or licenses also must be verified. Finally, all offers of employment should be made conditional upon successful completion of these checks.

G. Handling Reference Checks from Potential Employers; Duty To Warn

On the flip side of the coin, issues of potential liability arise when an educational institution dismisses a teacher, or the teacher resigns amidst allegations or proof of sexual harassment, abuse and the like. It is not unusual for the institution, as well as the harasser and the harassee, to maintain a low-key, low publicity approach. Oftentimes, institutions will enter into a settlement agreement in which resignation is traded for a confidentiality provision. Institutions should carefully consider the potential liability before entering into such an agreement. When negotiating agreements with accused employees regarding inquiries from prospective employees, hiding substantial information and evidence may not be appropriate and may be unlawful.[121]

Educators receiving inquiries about former employees face potential liability for defamation, but on the other hand, the institution

---

121. For example, in Ohio, one appellate court has held that a confidential settlement agreement between a school and teacher accused of child abuse was unenforceable for violating public policy. Bowman v. Parma Bd. of Educ., 44 Ohio App. 3d 169 (1988) (teacher was suing district for breach of the confidentiality provision; agreement held unenforceable because it impacted the weakest more vulnerable sector of the public).

also may face ethical issues or liability for failing to release important information related to sexual harassment, abuse or other discrimination. Generally speaking, institutions should release information and facts to prospective employers about sexual impropriety or resignation in face of sexual misconduct, but they must be sure the information accurate and conforms with applicable agreements or laws. State reporting statutes may relieve the institution from making such hard decisions where they are required to report certain crimes such as child abuse or felonies.[122] If the school intends not release such information as a matter of policy or practice applicable in every situation, it must first determine potential liability for such policy or practice.

Thus far, courts have refused to recognize suits brought against an educational institution as a former employer based upon an alleged duty to warn the new employer of the employee's propensity toward sexual harassment and the like.[123] Nevertheless, the courts may eventually recognize such a duty. For example, in April, 1992, the trustees for the La Jolla Country Day school filed suit against the University School in Milwaukee, Wisconsin, another private school, alleging that it failed to disclose allegations of sexual harassment against its former headmaster, Littleford.[124] La Jolla suspended the headmaster after a receptionist filed sexual harassment charges alleging inappropriate touching and comments, and that he pressured her for a date.[125] Educators must be mindful that students and parents are becoming more aware of their rights and willing to attempt to assert them. Several publications, for example, are specifically directed toward the student population students to alert them of sexual harassment.[126] In sum, given the potential liability under Title IX, other federal law, state statutes or common law, educational institutions are well advised to attempt to prevent and remedy sexual harassment of its students.

---

122. For example, the OHIO REVISED CODE requires schools to report child abuse, R.C. § 2151.421, and felonies, R.C. § 2921.22(A).

123. *See, e.g.*, Cohen v. Wales, 518 N.Y.S.2d 633 (N.Y. Ct. App. 1987) (rejected duty to warn theory where former employee had been charged with sexual misconduct because no special relationship existed between the district and the employee or with the alleged victim as required by Tarasoff v. Regents of the Univ. of Cal., 17 Cal. 3d 425, 551 P.2d 334, 131 Cal. Rptr. 14 (1976) (en banc))

124. Granberry, *Country Day Sues In Headmaster's Hiring*, L.A. Times, Apr. 24, 1992, Metro Section, at 1, pt. B, col. 4.

125. *Id*

126. These publications include, for example, a U.S. Department of Education, Office of Civil Rights, pamphlet called SEXUAL HARASSMENT: IT'S NOT ACADEMIC (1991); a program and workbook for teens called SEXUAL HARASSMENT AND TEENS by Susan Straus (Free Spirit Publishing, 1992); and a University of Michigan booklet entitled TUNE IN TO YOUR RIGHTS: A GUIDE FOR TEENAGERS ABOUT TURNING OFF SEXUAL HARASSMENT (1985).

VII. PREPARING FOR AND HANDLING SEXUAL HARASSMENT CLAIMS

A. Insurance Concerns

The time to check the institution's insurance policy for potential coverage is *before* a claim arises. Check your insurance policy to see what is or is not covered, i.e., child abuse, sexual harassment, negligent supervision? Who is covered, i.e., the district, board members, administrators? Will the insurance carrier indemnify in the event of liability? Will the carrier defend, even if it will not indemnify?

Finally, if the institution is put on notice that a claim may be made, notify the insurance carrier immediately. Many policies contain provisions requiring such notification to gain coverage.

B. Publicity Concerns

In cases of sexual harassment, abuse and discrimination, the public confidence is crucial. Once again, the institution must take action *before* a claim arises to develop a policy and procedure for handling publicity of such matters. Careful regulation of publicity will minimize trauma to victims, and insure fairness and privacy to the accused. A statement from the institution may be necessary especially in serious cases because "lack of official response is often misconstrued as approval or lack of concern."[127]

Disclosure of harassment of a student may also give rise to an obligation to report the conduct to a law enforcement agency or a children's services agency. Oftentimes, the failure to do so will result in a criminal offense.

C. Avoiding Liability for Sexual Harassment

Several factors play an important role in dispelling employer liability, including the presence or absence of an effective policy which specifically addresses sexual harassment, not mere discrimination. *Many courts have found the key determination in cases of sexual harassment is the presence or absence of an effective, publicized and consistently enforced sexual harassment policy and complaint pro-*

---

127. Hughes, *supra* note 75, at 10.

cedure.[128] A similar rule of thumb will no doubt prove influential in the student harassment context.

The educational institution's responsiveness may also alleviate liability for injuries that occur despite its efforts to remedy the situation. Moreover, where an employer investigates an employee's complaints, and disciplines and demotes the harasser, it may not be liable for residual emotional distress suffered by the victim of harassment.[129] Likewise, if the employer takes immediate and reasonable action to correct the situation, it may be absolved of liability.[130]

For example, in *Kauffman v. Allied Signal, Inc.*,[131] the Sixth Court found no employer liability where "its response upon learning of [the] harassment was adequate and effective." The offending supervisor fired a female machine operator after she rebuffed his attempts to touch her surgically enlarged breasts, attempts to look down her shirt and requests to see her new breasts. The employer's response of creating a sexual harassment policy *ex ante* and firing the supervisor was found to be "adequate and effective."

Similarly, in *Hirschfeld v. New Mexico Corrections Dept.*,[132] a typist complained after she was approached by a correctional officer on several occasions and was hugged and kissed. The employer took immediate action, including suspending the officer pending an investigation and ultimately demoting him. Because the employer took prompt and appropriate corrective action in dealing with the harassment, the court concluded the employer was not liable for the typist's residual depression.

Similarly, in the student context, Title IX clearly provides that recipients of federal funds must establish and publish procedures encompassing complaints of sexual harassment including its "prompt and equitable" resolution.[133]

The need for every educational institution to have an effective sexual harassment policy and reporting procedure are readily appar-

---

128. Meritor Sav. Bank v. Vinson, 477 U.S. 57 (1986); Kauffman v. Allied Signal, Inc., 970 F.2d 178 (6th Cir. 1992); Carrero v. New York City Hous. Auth., 890 F.2d 569 (2d Cir. 1989); Andrews v. City of Philadelphia, 895 F.2d 1469 (3d Cir. 1990); Neely v. Grenada, 799 F.2d 203 (5th Cir. 1986); Waltman v. International Paper Co., 875 F.2d 468 (5th Cir. 1989); Steele v. Offshore Shipbuilding, Inc., 867 F.2d 1311 (11th Cir. 1989).

129. *See, e.g.*, Hirschfeld v. New Mexico Corrections Dep't, 916 F.2d 572 (10th Cir. 1990).

130. Kirkland v. Brinias d/b/a Original Louis Drive-In Restaurant, 741 F. Supp. 692 (E.D. Tenn. 1990) (under the EEOC Guidelines, the employer may be absolved of liability if it takes immediate and appropriate corrective action). *See* Shager v. Upjohn Co., 913 F.2d 398 (7th Cir. 1990); Rabidue v. Osceola Refining Co., 805 F.2d 611 (6th Cir. 1986).

131. 970 F.2d 178 (6th Cir. 1992).

132. 916 F.2d 572 (10th Cir. 1990).

133. 34 C.F.R. 106.8.

ent. A federal district court in New Jersey, for example, held a municipal employer that failed to take steps to prevent sexual harassment and failed to encourage reporting of harassment, may be liable for its deliberate indifference to the possibility of harassment *even where the employer was unaware of any sexual harassment.*[134] The court boldly stated that the "risk of sexual harassment in the workplace is so obvious that an employer's failure to take action to prevent or stop it from occurring — *even in the absence of actual knowledge of its occurrence* — constitutes deliberate indifference, where the employer has also failed to take any steps to encourage the reporting of such incidents."[135] With that, educational institutions cannot expect to avoid liability for sexual harassment in the absence of a formal written policy specifically against sexual harassment and an effective reporting procedure. (See Appendix C).

1. Adopt a Written Policy

In today's world, reliance on a general antidiscrimination policy may not insulate an educational institution from liability. Educational institutions must establish a written policy against sexual harassment which applies to its employees and students. (See Appendices E, F, and G). The policy should describe or give a definition of sexual harassment, specifically state conduct which is forbidden and give examples of harassing behavior. Institutions may want to include a general cover-all category as well, for example, any act based upon a lack of respect for others.[136]

The policy should also set forth a reporting procedure for complaints and require that complaints be reported. The policy should establish and maintain open lines of communication with educators, administrators and students. It should encourage individuals to report violations. The name of the person to whom reports should be made must be widely disseminated. Assurances of confidentiality, to the greatest degree possible, will also increase reporting.[137]

The policy should declare that all complaints will be immediately investigated and that discipline, up to and including discharge, will be imposed for violations of the policy. The institution may want to include a provision in its policy which would empower it to pursue claims even if a student does not report a complaint or does not want

---

134. *See, e.g.*, Reynolds v. Avalon New Jersey, 59 F.E.P. Cases 1049 (D.C. N.J., Aug. 5, 1992).

135. *Id.*

136. Hughes, *supra* note 75, at 10.

137. *Id.* at 11.

to pursue a complaint. In doing so, institutions will wish to weigh the chilling effect of language that forces or permits it to pursue the claim.

As such policies affect terms and conditions of employment, they will be subject to collective bargaining obligations, where they affect bargaining unit members.

Likewise, student handbooks or codes of conduct must include sexual harassment as prohibited conduct. Not only should the code reflect the institution's policy definition of harassment, it should clearly spell out the potential consequences of a violation. The failure to do so may result in violation of the offending student's right to due process.

2. Establish a Reporting Procedure

The reporting procedure should include at least two lines of authority for meaningful reporting in order to insulate the institution from liability. The institution will not receive the beneficial impact of having and using such a policy if the perpetrator is charged with taking complaints or the institution is shown not to encourage victims of harassment to come forward.[138] Whoever is charged with receiving complaints must receive them seriously and err on the side of prudishness. Sarcasm or other non-serious behavior displayed to the reporting victim will haunt an institution which later attempts to defend itself from claims of discrimination.[139]

The policy may include components of informal as well as formal reporting of complaints. Informal reporting procedures are particularly helpful where the victim and the accused do not want publicity on the matter. If complaints are handled informally, the accused can agree to a penalty, apologize to the victim and avoid widespread publicity, investigation and other proceedings.[140] In such a case, where the student simply wants the harassment to stop, a letter technique has been recommended in order to empower the victim.[141] The victim writes a letter giving a factual account of what happened, how it

---

138. Meritor Sav. Bank v. Vinson, 477 U.S. 57, 73 (1986); *see, e.g.*, Neely v. Grenada, 799 F.2d 203 (5th Cir. 1986) (employer is not shielded from liability by plaintiff's failure to use a grievance procedure where the first step in the procedure was to complain to the harassing supervisor).

139. *See, e.g.*, Waltman v. International Paper Co., 875 F.2d 468 (5th Cir. 1989) (summary judgment for the employer was reversed on appeal on the basis of whether sufficient remedial action was taken).

140. Hughes, *supra* note 75, at 10.

141. *Id.*

made the victim feel, and an affirmative statement of what the victim wants, i.e., the harassment to stop.[142]

3. Educate Supervisors, Employees and Students of the Policy and Reporting Procedure

At the very least the sexual harassment policy must be posted and distributed to all supervisors, employees and students. The policy should be posted in all appropriate places including employee and student lunch rooms, hallways, bulletin boards, teacher lounges, the employee handbook and affirmative action plan. It should be disseminated, and redisseminated, on a regular basis. Supervisors, employees and students must be periodically reminded of the policy and reporting procedure.

All supervisors and teachers must also be reminded that they are the eyes and ears of the institution and must be on the lookout for harassment. Supervisors and employees must immediately advise the institution of any complaints of sexual harassment received by them or potential harassment witnessed by them. Even employees who have no supervisory function may be responsible to notify other educators or administrators or the Board of harassing behavior, particularly between students. This may well include janitorial personnel who become aware of sexually harassing graffiti on a bathroom wall. Likewise, it could include a faculty member who knows or should know of harassment but does nothing to stop it.[143] Finally, these same individuals should be reassured that good faith reporting of harassment and taking part in an investigation will not result in adverse employment or disciplinary action.

Educational institutions should consider conducting workshops or in- service programs regarding sexual harassment and the policy on an annual basis. Periodic or regular newsletters distributed to employees and students could contain additional information regarding the policy, reporting procedure or harassment. As a rule of thumb, the more efforts that are taken to educate and inform the educational population of harassment and the policy against it, the greater the likelihood that the institution will be absolved of liability for harassment. Today, it is unlikely an educational institution can avoid liability for harassment without taking some effort to adopt and utilize a formal harassment policy and effective reporting procedure.

---

142. *Id.* (citing Writing A Letter To The Harasser, Project on the Status and Education of Women, Association of American Colleges).

143. *Id.* at 8.

Education may also be achieved through a review of peer harassment issues in open hearings, interviews, and evaluations.[144] Institutions should encourage student organizations and student government to pass harassment resolutions.[145] Moreover, institutions should develop a method to inspect grounds, including desk top graffiti, for harassing statements and develop a procedure to remove it and remedy it as soon as possible.[146]

4. Dealing with Complaints and Conducting Investigations

Investigations must be conducted immediately. (See Appendix D). The alleged harasser must be advised that retaliation or contact with the victim by him/her or friends will not be accepted and subject to penalty.[147] In student cases, it may be appropriate to inform both sets of parents.[148] Institutions should respond appropriately to anonymous reports of harassment. Depending on the seriousness of the allegations, such a response may include talking to the alleged harasser or conducting a full-scale investigation.[149]

It is essential that complaints of sexual harassment be treated in a confidential manner which take into account the sensitive nature of the allegation for both the alleged harasser and the alleged victim. Information regarding the allegations should be shared only with those who need to know. Even if a conclusion is reached that the victim has been sexually harassed, it is rarely necessary to broadcast that fact.

Prompt and immediate corrective action is the rule to live by for educational institutions because courts have ruled time and again that prompt and immediate corrective action precludes or mitigates liability for harassment in the employment context.[150]

Documentation of the investigation is very important because it is often the only contemporaneous evidence of the allegations, the knowledge and credibility of witnesses, and the employer's efforts to remedy the problem. The investigation should include interviews of the victim and the alleged harasser, and written and/or sworn statements from both. The alleged harasser should be given the opportu-

---

144. *Id.* at 10.

145. *Id.* at 11.

146. *Id.*

147. *Id.* at 12.

148. *Id.*

149. *Id.* at 11.

150. *See, e.g.*, Steele v. Offshore Shipbuilding, Inc., 867 F.2d 1311 (11th Cir. 1989); Swentek v. U.S. Air, Inc., 830 F.2d 552 (4th Cir. 1987).

nity to respond to the allegations and provide his/her side of the story and rebutting evidence. Other interviews should include those witnesses with knowledge of a particular relevant incident, other similar incidents involving the parties or either of them, and witnesses who can vouch for the good character of the alleged harasser. Above all else, flexibility is necessary in the investigation as all cases will require special attention to different details.

The investigator must keep track of all investigatory efforts including all leads, interviews and telephone calls. For example, records must be kept even if a lead or interview failed to reveal information relevant to the allegations. Remember, the employer's efforts to promptly and effectively investigate and remedy the allegations is a key mitigating factor in court.

Finally, the investigator should keep the victim and, where appropriate, the victim's parents apprised of efforts made throughout the investigation, and both parties should be informed when a determination is made.

5. Corrective Action

If the institution concludes that sexual harassment occurred, discipline of the offending employee or student is usually appropriate. In the employment context, discharge may be appropriate depending on the egregiousness of the offense. However, at least one court has implied that discharge is too harsh where an employer has no sexual harassment policy or has a policy which fails to clearly state that a first time offense of sexual harassment may be a dischargeable offense.[151] (That is why the sexual harassment policy must include that discharge for the first offense as a possible ramification). Verbal reprimand, transfer, demotion or discharge, however, may also be appropriate based on the facts of each separate case. Institutions should feel confident in taking such action as no court has recognized an alleged harasser's claim for "reverse sex discrimination" under Title VII because he is fired out of the employer's fear of being sued by the victim, even where the harasser claims that the employer failed to properly investigate the charges.[152]

Similarly, in the student context, the policy or code of conduct must specifically set forth a range of remedies and/or penalties, and indicate retaliation for bringing a complaint is actionable. The

---

151. *See* Bush v. Metro Transit Auth., 51 F.E.P. Cases 1217 (D. Kan. 1989) (the fact that the harasser had been informed of his employer's policy against harassment legitimized his discharge for harassment).

152. *See, e.g.*, Coen v. Elco Chevrolet, Inc., 756 F. Supp. 414 (E.D. Mo. 1991).

accused may be required to get counselling, in addition to other penalties.[153] Sanctions may include group workshops, informing parents, requiring public service, writing an apology letter to victim, probation, suspension, or expulsion.[154] Naturally, institutions must comply with students' due process rights.

Merely punishing the harasser, however, may not be a sufficient remedy for harassment. The remedy may need to incorporate, for example, a benefit to the victim. If the victim has been discharged, demoted or failed to be promoted because of sexual harassment, the victim should be reemployed, put back to her position, or promoted. Reassigning or moving the victim may also be appropriate under certain circumstances.[155]

The remedy may also include in-service or workshop activities particularly if focused on a group of employees or students affected by the particular harassing situation. The remedy may also include creating or beefing up the policy or procedures for dealing with harassment, further educating employees, supervisors and/students regarding the policy or harassment, or other creative solutions tailored to the specific situation. In sum, when dispensing corrective action or remedies, flexibility, again, is the key. No one remedy will cure all harassment or shield an institution from liability.

---

153. *Id.* at 12.

154. *Id.*

155. *See, e.g.*, Guess v. Bethlehem Steel Corp., 913 F.2d 463 (7th Cir. 1990) (harassed employee had been assigned only temporarily to work under the guilty foreman who was disciplined with reprimand, warning to stay away from the female employee and later denial of promotion and merit increase).

APPENDIX A

FEDERAL AVENUES TO LIABILITY FOR SEXUAL HARASSMENT IN EDUCATION

Entitlement	Who Can Sue	Nature of Liability	Jury	Remedies	Statute of Limitations
Title VII of the Civil Rights Act, 42 U.S.C. §§ 2000e, *et seq.*	Employees	Private and public institutional liability for acts of supervisors and employees for *quid pro quo* and hostile environment harassment	Yes, under Civil Rights Act of 1991 for discriminatory acts occurring on or after Nov. 7, 1991	Injunctive relief for discriminatory acts occurring prior to Nov. 7, 1991 for acts occurring after Nov. 7, 1991, compensatory damages and, if malicious, punitive damages of $50,000 to $300,000	180 days to file charge with EEOC (300 days in deferral state); 90 days to sue in court upon receipt of notice of right to sue
Civil Rights Act of 1991, 42 U.S.C. § 1981	Employees	Same as above	Same as above	Same as above	Same as above
Title IX of the Education Amendments of 1974 20 U.S.C. § 1681. *et seq.*	Employees and students	Private and public institutional liability for sexual harassment of students or employees in programs/institutions receiving federal funds	Yes	Compensatory damages and injunctive relief	Borrow from state statute of limitations for similar cause of action, usually personal injury
42 U.S.C. § 1983	Employees and students	Public institutional and individual liability where there is a policy of sexual harassment under "color of state law"	Yes	Compensatory and punitive damages, and injunctive relief	Determined by state statute of limitations applicable to personal injury cases
United States Constitution – Equal Protection Clause of the 14th Amendment	Employees and students	Public institutional liability for intentional sexual harassment	Yes	Compensatory and punitive damages, and injunctive relief	Determined by state statute of limitations applicable to personal injury cases

APPENDIX B

TYPES OF SEXUAL HARASSMENT IN EMPLOYMENT

***Quid Pro Quo* Harassment** occurs when submission to OR rejection of sexual advances/requests is used as the basis for employment.

Example: Professor requests sex from another professor in exchange for a recommendation for tenure and, after his advances are spurned, he recommends denial of tenure.

Remember: - one single incident may create educational institution liability

- an educational institution is liable for acts of its supervisors even if unaware such acts occurred

Hostile Environment Harassment occurs when unwelcome, severe and pervasive sexual conduct that unreasonably interferes with an individual's job performance or creates an intimidating, hostile or offensive working environment.

Example: Transportation Director tells sexual jokes, touches female bus driver on the breast, and corners her when she is alone on a bus before her run.

Remember: - the intent of the harasser does not matter — the test for harassment is from the viewpoint of a reasonable woman and/or the actual victim

- an educational institution is liable for acts of its employees if it knows or should have known such acts occurred

APPENDIX C

CHECKLIST FOR PREVENTION OF LIABILITY

- Adopt a written sexual harassment policy

- Establish a reporting procedure

- Educate supervisors and employees of the policy and reporting procedure through workshops, newsletters, posting and passing out of the policy, roleplay, in-service

- Warn supervisors they are the eyes and ears of the institution; moreover, they are the institution

- encourage employees to report of suspected harassment

APPENDIX D

CHECKLIST FOR COMPLAINTS AND CONDUCTING INVESTIGATIONS

1. **Reporting**

   - Establish clear routes for reporting harassment

   - Establish more than one route for reporting harassment

   - Educate employees regarding the reporting routes

   - Encourage reporting of harassment

   - Tell supervisors they are the eyes and ears of the institution and cannot turn the other cheek

2. **Receiving Complaints**

   - The individual receiving complaints should talk personally with the suspected victim

   - Complaints should be reduced to writing, and a sworn statement should be taken if possible

   - Complaints should be held in confidence to the extent possible and as allowed by the law

   - Complainants should receive assurances that their good faith complaint and cooperation will not result in adverse employment action

   - Complainants should be referred to proper authorities when necessary; the authorities should be notified by institution representatives as well.

   - Consideration should be given to whether the seriousness of the complaint, the credibility of the victim and potential threat to others require immediate removal of the harasser from the workplace pending the outcome of a thorough investigation

3. **Conducting an Investigation**

   - Investigations should be held in confidence to the extent possible and as allowed by law

   - Investigations must be prompt and thorough

   - The alleged harasser must be personally interviewed and a written/sworn statement taken if possible. The harasser should be confronted with all allegations and allowed the opportunity to respond to each.

   - Witnesses should be interviewed and written statements taken. Witness may also include others who can attest to the nature of the alleged harasser whether or not they support the allegations or harassment.

   - Written notes must be kept of all efforts made to investigate the alleged harassment

4. **The Results**

   - Depending on whether or not sexual harassment is found, the nature and seriousness of the harassment which is found, applicable collective bargaining agreements, policies, practices and law, an educational institution may take several actions.

   - Such actions likely included discipline of the harasser including termination for the first offense

   - A court may not find disciplining the harasser a sufficient remedy to circumvent liability on the part of the educational institution; thus, further remedial action may be necessary

   - Give a benefit to the victim

   - Conduct an inservice for others potentially affected by the harassment

APPENDIX E

[SAMPLE POLICY FOR HARASSMENT AT SECONDARY SCHOOL LEVEL]

PROHIBITION OF HARASSMENT

Federal and state law prohibit racial, ethnic, religious, age or sexual harassment of any employee or student. Furthermore, such conduct is offensive, unprofessional and sets a poor example for our students and community. Accordingly, the Board of Education will not tolerate harassment and will make every effort to maintain schools free from harassment.

Racial, ethnic, religious and age harassment includes such conduct as slurs, jokes, intimidation, or any other verbal or physical attack directed at an individual's race, religion, national origin or age.

Sexual harassment includes unwelcome sexual advances, requests for sexual favors, and other verbal or physical conduct of a sexual nature when:

1. Submission to such conduct is an explicit or implicit term or condition of an individual's employment or participation in a school-related activity; or,

2. Submission to or rejection of such conduct by an individual is used as the basis for employment decisions or grades affecting the individual; or,

3. Such conduct has the purpose or effect of unreasonably interfering with the individual's work or school performance or creating an intimidating, hostile, or offensive work or school environment.

In order for the Board of Education to effectively enforce this policy and to take prompt, corrective measures, it is essential that any and all incidents of harassment be reported to your building principal, Directorof SpecialEducation/Psychologist, and/or the Superintendent. Verbal complaints will be reduced to writing to assist the Board of Education's investigation. To the greatest extent possible, such complaints will be treated in a confidential manner. Limited disclosure may be necessary in order to complete a thorough investigation.

If, after appropriate investigation, the Board of Education finds that an employee has violated this policy, prompt corrective action will be taken in accordance with the applicable collective bargaining agreement(s), Board policy and/or state law.

APPENDIX F

[SAMPLE POLICY]

POLICY AGAINST HARASSMENT

Policy

The Board of Education actively endorses the principle and spirit of Equal Opportunity in Employment, it is a policy of this Board to recruit, hire, train, pay, promote, discipline, provide benefits and maintain all other conditions of employment in accordance with applicable federal, state and local law without regard to sex, color, race, national origin, religion, age or disability. Moreover, it is a policy of this Board not to tolerate verbal or physical conduct by any person who harasses, disrupts or interferes with another's work or educational environment, or which creates an intimidating, offensive or hostile work or educational environment.

While all forms of harassment are prohibited, the Board's policy is to specifically prohibit sexual harassment. Each School District employee has a responsibility to maintain a workplace and educational environment free from harassment. Harassment or offensive conduct in the workplace is prohibited. For purposes of this policy, harassment includes, but is not limited to, intimidation or persistent abuse of another, whether physically, orally or in writing.

Sexual harassment may include unwelcome sexual advances, requests for sexual favors or other verbal or physical conduct of a sexual nature where:

1. Submission to such conduct is made either explicitly or implicitly a term or condition of a person's employment or educational development;

2. Submission to or rejection of such conduct is used as the basis for employment or education decisions affecting such individual, or

3. Such conduct has a purpose or effect of unreasonably interfering with an individual's work or educational performance, or creating an intimidating, hostile or offensive working or educational environment.

Specifically, sexual harassment may include, but is not limited to:

1. Sexual flirtations, touching, advances or propositions;
2. Verbal or physical abuse of a sexual nature;

3. Graphic or suggestive comments about an individual's dress or body;

4. Sexually degrading words to describe an individual;

5. Displaying sexually aggressive objects or photographs; and/or

6. Sexually explicit or obscene jokes.

It is Board policy that all reports of harassment will thoroughly investigated, and violations of this policy will be treated as serious disciplinary infractions. No employee shall be subjected to adverse employment action in retaliation for any good faith report of harassment or participating in an investigation about harassment under this policy. To the extent possible, all reports of harassment will be kept confidential.

Procedure

1. Any person who believes he or she has been subjected to sexually or otherwise harassing behavior by another person is encouraged to confront the offender in an effort to stop the offensive behavior.

2. Any person who believes he or she has been subjected to harassment must promptly report the alleged harassment to his or her administrator. If the complaint involves the administrator, such report should be made to the Executive Director or Assistant Director of Human Resources.

3. Administrators who receive a complaint alleging harassment must report such complaint promptly to the Executive Director or Assistant Director of Human Resources.

4. The Executive Director or Assistant Director of Human Resources will consider the truth and veracity of the complaint. The Executive Director or Assistant Director of Human Resources will promptly and confidentially begin an investigation which may include some or all of the following steps:

   (a) The Executive Director of Human Resources or his or her designee will confer with the complainant to obtain a clear understanding of the of facts surrounding the allegation of harassment.

   (b) The Executive Director of Human Resources or his or her designee will then give the accused person the opportunity to confer and obtain his or her version of the incident(s).

   (c) The Executive Director of Human Resources or his or her designee may hold as many meetings with the alleged victim and accused as are necessary to investigate the complaint. In addition, the Executive Director or his or her designee may meet with any witnesses to the alleged harassment.

(d) In all cases, the employee shall be informed of the general results of the investigation by the Executive Director of Human Resources or his or her designee.

5. On the basis of the investigation, the Executive Director of Human Resources or his or her designee may do any of the following:

(a) resolve the matter informally;

(b) report the entire matter to the Superintendent; and/or

(c) recommend to the Superintendent disciplinary action up to an including discharge.

6. It is the responsibility of the Superintendent to determine what further action should be taken on a complaint of harassment after receiving a recommendation of disciplinary action from the Executive Director of Human Resources or his or her designee. The Superintendent may then do any of the following:

(a) conduct an independent investigation;

(b) resolve the matter informally;

(c) report the entire matter to the Board of Education, and/or

(d) recommend to the Board of Education disciplinary action up to and including discharge.

7. The Executive Director of Human Resources will periodically review this policy.

8. The Executive Director of Human Resources shall have this Policy posted to inform School District employees about it.

Adopted by the Board of Education on _________________________.

APPENDIX G

[SAMPLE POLICY]

STUDENT CODE OF CONDUCT — PROHIBITION AGAINST SEXUAL HARASSMENT

Students who engage in sexual harassment on school premises or off school premises at a school-sponsored activity will be subject to appropriate discipline, including suspension or expulsion. Sexual harassment is any activity of a sexual nature that is unwanted or unwelcome, including but not limited to, unwanted touching, pinching, patting, verbal comments of a sexual nature, sexual name-calling, pressure to engage sexual activity, repeated propositions, and unwanted body contact. The school's normal disciplinary procedures will be followed in determining the appropriate consequence for the sexual harassment. In the event the administration recommends suspension or expulsion as a result of the conduct, due process will be afforded to the student in accordance with the district's suspension/expulsion procedures.

APPENDIX H

TYPICAL FORMS OF SEXUAL HARASSMENT IN EMPLOYMENT

Verbal	Visual	Physical
telling sexual jokes	wearing suggestive attire	touching, making physical contact
asking for sexual favors	staring at another's anatomy	standing too close
comments about another's anatomy	flirting/suggestive eye contact	"too lengthy" handshake
pursuing an unwanted relationship	sitting in a suggestive position	touching or brushing another's clothing
compliments with sexual overtones	circulating sexual jokes, cartoons, pornography	preventing another from leaving an area
perpetuating sex — based stereotypes	making sexual hand gestures	requiring another to pick something up off the floor, walk across the room

APPENDIX I

COSTS OF SEXUAL HARASSMENT IN EMPLOYMENT

Victims of sexual harassment:

- focus on avoiding the harasser not on work, education, students, creativity, contribution to faculty projects, contributions to extra projects

- experience high anxiety, destroyed confidence, physical and psychological illness

- are absent more often

- are less likely to be promoted, receive tenure

- seek legal recourse

Educational institutions with sexual harassment within the ranks:

- experience increased turnover among employees

- experience higher absenteeism among employees

- are subject to negative employee morale

- are subject to negative publicity

- are subject to lawsuits and grievances, and resulting liability and legal fees

- experience spill-over which affects education and student attitudes

APPENDIX J

FAVORITISM AND ROMANCE IN THE WORKPLACE

Guidelines

- isolated instances of favoritism towards a "paramour" are not prohibited

- favoritism based upon coerced sexual conduct may constitute *quid pro quo* harassment

- widespread favoritism may constitute hostile environment harassment

Prevention

- bans on co-worker dating are legal in most states

- employers may legitimately distinguish between social and sexual fraternizing

- many state laws allow anti-nepotism policies as long as they are applied equally to both sexes